Jumpstart Your LinkedIn™ Profile:
67 Actionable Tips

By

Sandra Long

Copyright 2024 by Sandra Long

All rights reserved. Published 2024.

No portion of this book may be reproduced in any form or by any means without the publisher's prior written permission, except for brief quotations embodied in critical reviews and certain other noncommercial uses permitted by copyright law.

ISBN Paperback: 979-8-9884775-0-1
ISBN Digital: 979-8-9884775-1-8

Cover Design by ebooklaunch.com

Publisher: Pro Tip Press

Printed in the United States of America

1st Printing, 2024

DISCLAIMER

LinkedIn™ is the registered trademark of LinkedIn Corporation or its affiliates. The use of the LinkedIn trademark in connection with this product does not signify any affiliation with or endorsement by LinkedIn Corporation or its affiliates.

BULK ORDERS

Jumpstart Your LinkedIn™ Profile: 67 Actionable Tips is available at special discounts when purchased in bulk through the author. Also, consider ordering special editions or book excerpts. For details, contact Sandra@PostRoadConsulting.com.

Sandra Long
PO Box 381
Epping, NH 03833

Praise for
"Jumpstart Your LinkedIn Profile"

As one of the top LinkedIn experts in the world, Sandra Long has always been my go-to person for all things LinkedIn-related. In her excellent first book, she showed us how to build a more memorable and powerful personal brand. And now, in her wonderful new book, she walks us through the latest and greatest features and benefits to show how to Jumpstart Your LinkedIn™ Profile! Following Sandra's insightful advice, I have grown my LinkedIn network from 3,000 connections to 12,000 over the past 5 years, leading to many wonderful new relationships and opening the doors to numerous fantastic new business opportunities. And after applying many of the actionable tips in this book, I look forward to taking my LinkedIn profile to a whole new level.

Todd Cherches
CEO and Executive Coach, BigBlueGumball. Adjunct Professor of Leadership at NYU and Columbia University. Author of "VisuaLeadership"

I teach LinkedIn strategies to college students, and these well-researched tips and suggestions are what everyone needs to know, to make their profiles stand out for all the right reasons! With examples and action steps throughout the book, you will be able to follow along and craft your compelling message.

Beth Settje
Associate Director, UConn Center for Career Development

Sandra has captured in one place all the most salient tips for creating and maintaining an impactful LinkedIn profile and presence. As a corporate TA leader responsible for over 100,000 hires a year, I can't overstate the importance of investing sufficient time and effort in this space, whether you're actively looking for work or simply building your professional network. With practical tips, action items and detailed illustrations, Sandra's book is a comprehensive resource that will help readers put their best foot forward and truly stand out on this critical platform.

Dan Black
EY Global Leader of Talent Attraction and Acquisition

Jumpstart your LinkedIn profile is a crucial read for anyone looking to stand out on LinkedIn. It provides a comprehensive but yet clear-cut roadmap to build your presence, enhance your visibility, and achieve notoriety in the platform—teaching you how to capitalize on every single profile feature for your benefit. Sandra's practical approach to their books is a gem, and this is no exception—she simplifies your learning journey with a book packaged with actionable tips that will make you log into LinkedIn immediately.

Alvaro Bendrell
Director of Digital Communications at Enel North America

The quintessential guide to your LinkedIn profile. If you want to gain the respect of your peers on LinkedIn, read and apply. If you're looking for clients, a career change, or share your company values as an ambassador, this is the book for you.

Luca Bozzato
CEO @ In Consulting, 1st Italian Certified LinkedIn Consultant. Host of the "LinkedIn Mindset" podcast.

Sandra's book provides an up-to-date primer for anyone looking to optimize their LinkedIn profile. Written in an easy-to-follow style and accompanied by clear "action steps" for each bit of advice, this is an excellent guide to jumpstart your LinkedIn presence.

John Espirian
Relentlessly helpful® LinkedIn nerd. Author of "Content DNA"

I look forward to using this book in our "Building Your Career Brand" course with my students. Sandra is a favorite guest speaker in my classes. With her books and talks, she inspires our students every time!

Gail Lowney Alofsin
Keynote Speaker, Author, and Professor at the University of Rhode Island

Your dream clients are on LinkedIn. This book helps you put your best foot forward in capturing their attention without draining yours. It's quick, simple, and delightfully practical. Sandra Long has done it again!

Bill Soroka
Best-selling author and serial entrepreneur.

Sandra's book is an easy and quick read that is packed with useful tips and suggestions on how to make your LinkedIn profile more informative and useful for your connections. What I love about her tips is that she explains "why and how" in a way that any generation can benefit from her guidance. The reader can actually do something today that will have an immediate impact tomorrow.

Michael Pitcher
Former CEO of LeasePlan USA, Professional Speaker. Author of "Seven eLements of Leadership for a New Breed of Leader."

Sandra Long's "Jumpstart your LinkedIn Profile" offers practical advice for achieving your professional goals on LinkedIn, as well as actionable tips for building and strengthening your presence on LinkedIn.

Gwen Acton, PhD
CEO, Vivo Group

Sandra's book is a gold mine of smart and actionable tips. Keep it close to you for inspiration.

Leonardo Bellini
LinkedIn Trainer. Author of 2 LinkedIn Books.

Table of Contents

INTRODUCTION 1

POSITION YOURSELF 3
    1. Your Personal Brand 3
    2. Personalize Even More 5
    3. Identify Your Ideal Profile Viewer 6
    4. First Impressions Matter 7
    5. Artificial to Authentic 8
    6. Pivot 10
    7. Multi-Faceted Professional 11
    8. Open to Work: Active or Passive? 12
    9. Hiring Profile 13
    10. Selling Profile 15

POWERFUL PROSE 17
    11. Amazing and Proud, Not Boastful 17
    12. Write in the First Person 18
    13. Be Specific 18
    14. The Magic of Keywords 19
    15. Unique Ways to Find Keywords, Phrases, and Skills .. 20
    16. Avoid These Words and Phrases 22
    17. Ready, Set, Action 23
    18. Your About Essay–Be Interesting 23
    19. Powerful Headline 25
    20. Multilingual Capabilities 26

MORE PROFILE SECTIONS 28
    21. Work Experience 28
    22. Career Break or Not Currently Working? 29
    23. Add and Accentuate Skills 31

- 24. Endorsements 32
- 25. Your Learning Brand 33
- 26. Leverage the Services Page 34
- 27. Be Easy to Contact 35
- 28. Credibility-Boosting Sections 37

VISUAL VITALITY 38

- 29. Smile 38
- 30. Background Photo (Banner) Ideas 39
- 31. Sourcing Images the Right Way 41
- 32. Sizzling Multimedia Profile 42
- 33. Leverage Additional Media 44
- 34. White Space 45
- 35. Emojis or No? 45
- 36. Create a Custom Presentation 46

MORE WAYS TO BE FOUND 48

- 37. Complete Your Profile 48
- 38. Use the Name Field Properly 49
- 39. Customize Your URL 50
- 40. Optimize Your Location 51
- 41. Select Your Industry 52
- 42. Use Drop-Down Menus 53
- 43. Be Found via Google 54
- 44. Be Found via Your Network 55

SWEET SPOTS 57

- 45. Recommendations 57
- 46. Activity Spotlight 59
- 47. Distinguish Yourself as a Thought Leader 60
- 48. Drive Website Traffic 62

49. Add Audio Name Pronunciation 63
50. Add Gender Pronouns 64

TECHNICAL FOUNDATIONS 65

51. Profile Editing 65
52. Broadcast Your Profile Updates? 66
53. Download and Learn the Mobile App 66
54. Leverage the Profile QR Code 67
55. Profile Visibility Settings 69
56. Email Considerations 70
57. Security 70
58. Expand with Character 72
59. Quality Check 73

Closing Tips 74

60. Be the Friend First 74
61. Stay Professional 75
62. Evolving You 76
63. Slimming Down Your Profile 77
64. Brand Ambassador Opportunity 78
65. Add a Company Page and Logo 79
66. Compliance 80
67. Be Consistent 81

BONUS TIPS 82

68. Display and Share Your Profile 82
69. Increase Profile Views 83
70. It's Not a Tattoo! 84
71. Last Word for Job Seekers 84

MORE HELP IS HERE 86

ABOUT THE AUTHOR	**88**
BEFORE WE PART WAYS	**89**

INTRODUCTION

Welcome, dear reader! Whether you're stepping into LinkedIn for the first time or you're a seasoned user, this treasure trove of 67 LinkedIn profile tips is designed with you in mind.

Why am I sure you'll find value here? Because LinkedIn is a dynamic world, and we're all growing alongside it—professionally and personally. A regular rejuvenation of our profiles is not just beneficial; it's essential.

Imagine being part of the 50 million profiles discovered and reviewed each day on LinkedIn. Now, let's make sure when they're looking–they find you, and not just anyone, but the best professional version of you!

This tip book is crafted to be your go-to guide, packed with actionable insights and ideas. Don't forget to download the complimentary **Companion Guide** for deeper dives into key topics. You'll find the link at the end of this book. I call it "More Help is Here."

Discover the tips within the book sections, such as "Position Yourself," "Powerful Prose," and "Visual Vitality," among others. These tips will guide you to not only be found, but to stand out.

And if you're hungry for more LinkedIn advice, my international bestseller, *LinkedIn for Personal Branding: The Ultimate Guide*, awaits. It's a comprehensive masterclass combining LinkedIn strategies with personal branding expertise, including thought leadership, content creation, networking, and self-assessment strategies.

Welcome also to those readers of my *LinkedIn for Personal Branding* book or *Supercharge Your Notary Business with LinkedIn*! Use this as your refresher course, focusing on the latest in LinkedIn profile optimization.

I'd love to see you apply these 67-plus tips and triumph!

As I was writing, I included a few extra tips, so check out the bonus tips, too.

Connect with me on LinkedIn, share your progress, and let's keep the conversation going.

Ready to dive in with me? Let's embark on this journey to elevate your LinkedIn presence right now. Your next opportunity is just a tip away!

Sandra G. Long

POSITION YOURSELF

Tip #1

Your Personal Brand

Personal branding is the ongoing process of distinguishing yourself from others in your company, at your school, or in your industry. Today's successful professionals make a powerful impression and build valuable connections. I ask my clients, audiences, and readers this: "Consider how people currently know you and identify what you SHOULD be known for. What are the gaps?"

Beyond your experience, education, and expertise, what distinguishes you from others? How can you better highlight your values, vision, story, personality, or unique professional approach?

In my earlier book, *LinkedIn for Personal Branding*, I use the analogy of an orange fish among blue fish to emphasize the value of being your authentic self. Too many people present themselves in such a generic way (so many blue fish) that they have missed a key opportunity to differentiate themselves (orange fish).

Build a strong and friendly personal brand to enjoy increased recognition; more speaking, career, and business opportunities; and a reputation as an expert with a personal touch.

Here's an example for you. My good friend Gail Lowney Alofsin is a professional speaker and author. Yes, she's an expert. But Gail is also a connector, teacher, radio host, sales leader, and humanitarian who helps the extremely unfortunate among us. She is very optimistic and friendly, too. Her brand and reputation are based on all these factors, not just that she is a professional speaker and author. Her expertise, values, and personality all shine through. As a result, people trust and like her.

Most of us are not as multi-faceted as Gail, but consider just how you are unique. What is important to you? Even if you are just starting, why not focus on your learning journey or brand? If you are moving in a new direction career-wise or reinventing yourself, share that story and what is driving you. If you are a salesperson, how do you help customers? And if you are a corporate leader, what are your values?

Think big picture! Share what matters to you and people will respond.

Action Step: Jot down your unique approach, values, story, vision, experiences, expertise, interests, style, personal focus areas, favorite hashtags, and causes you care about. Write them down now. Keep them in mind as you begin profile updating and editing!

Tip #2

Personalize Even More

Include an element of YOU as a real person in your LinkedIn profile. Does this tip surprise you?

I had a new prospect at a large international company ask me about skiing because I mentioned it in the "fun" or "human" section of my profile. Hmmm, now we are talking about skiing and have a low-key personal common interest to share or discuss.

Are you a runner, sailor, or hiker? Do you enjoy cooking, yoga, or travel? Are you a loyal New England Patriots or *Seinfeld* fan?

Your professional contacts also have private lives with hobbies or interests. Sharing common interests is a great way to bond with someone who you wish to start a professional relationship with.

So yes, showcase your personality and personal interests. I subtly do this at the end of my About essay. Some people take their interests and make them a bigger part of their brand story. It depends on you.

> **Sandra's Sidebar**: I don't go overboard with personal information online. But it sure is nice to have an icebreaker at the ready. We are all human after all.

Action Step: Make a list of any personal interest items about yourself that you may want to weave into your profile. At the end of your About section, consider adding in your interests. (This is the third "H" of my "5H" About section format, which you will learn more about in Tip #18.)

Tip #3

Identify Your Ideal Profile Viewer

You want clarity in presenting yourself online. Your viewers need to know who you are; who your audience is; and how you solve their problems.

Who are you most interested in impressing on LinkedIn? Is it sales prospects, clients, partners, agents, candidates, employers, employees, members, volunteers, students, board members, or donors? Do you have a niche market?

Be sure to orient your profile as if you are speaking to that person or group of people.

Instead of talking only about yourself, be sure to include how you help or work with your ideal profile viewer. Your focus on this person or group can be a theme of your profile and brand.

Orient your profile so that your words address your ideal viewer. Your About, headline, Experience, Certifications, images, featured content, skills, etc. all provide you the opportunity to share your story of how you help this niche prospect.

You want your ideal reader to think, "This person is someone I need to know."

> **Sandra's Sidebar**: Clarity and focus on your ideal client will help you build trust with that particular person. Take it a step further and orient your content and engagement to appeal to that same target person.

Action Step: Write a detailed description of your ideal profile viewer and what they care about. Keep this description handy as you work on your profile. Too many profiles look like generic resumes. Don't let that be you.

Tip #4

First Impressions Matter

Establish an impressive ***Introduction Card*** that serves as your first impression. This is the "above-the-fold" section of your profile.

An effective profile motivates viewers to learn more and reach out to you. And it all starts at the very top—at the Intro Card. If you lose a viewer's interest there, they are unlikely to scroll down and read the rest, no matter how great it may be.

Make sure your Intro Card includes a professional-looking and clear profile picture. Choose an image that represents you well. Avoid using selfies or picture cut-outs. Write a meaningful headline including relevant keywords and/or the value you bring.

Your headline, photo, and banner are key to avoiding this mistake. The words and images should provide a unified look and feel that is strategic for your brand.

Premium users now have the option of adding a custom button on their Intro Card. Consider options such as visit my store; visit my website; view my portfolio; visit my blog; or book an appointment.

Sandra's Sidebar: You decide if you wish to display your school and company in your Intro Card. You can also select which school is showing. I recommend keeping both school and employer on display for most LinkedIn members. It is better for your networking and brand.

Action Step: Look at your Intro Card and make strategic decisions about what you wish to display. You have some flexibility in the images and the elements.

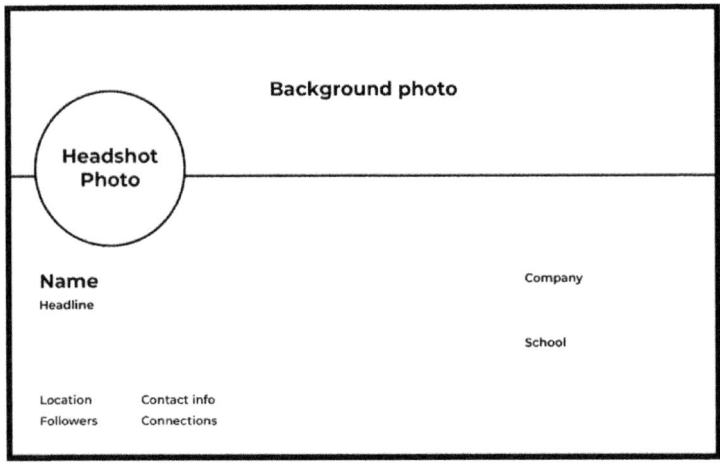

Tip #5

Artificial to Authentic

Artificial Intelligence is changing our world more than ever right now, but we need to be careful. AI allows us to save time and do our jobs more effectively. AI can help us with our LinkedIn profiles in the following ways:

- Summarize our descriptions or accomplishments
- Expand our descriptions.
- Identify keywords and phrases
- Reword or rephrase our About or Experience
- Create a new headshot
- Translate our profile
- and more!

But the fact is this...it is *our* job to be authentic. Don't just accept generic wording that was created by an Artificial Intelligence application. Use it as a tool to help you by spurring on ideas or cleaning up your copy.

Be yourself. Be *you*. Don't take AI content and use it word for word. Make it your own!

Here is my new A2A image I just created to help remind us to transform artificial to authentic.

Make it fun. Make it *you*.

Action Step: Experiment with AI as you work on your profile, but always make all words and phrases your own. Edit, adjust, and tweak any AI-generated profile content so that it is 100% authentic. Real people can tell the difference, so be real.

Tip #6

Pivot

Use LinkedIn to help pivot your career or business. Your profile is where people visit to learn about you. They are interested in you. Let's take out the confusion.

Share your journey and professional goals in the About section. Explain how you are learning, adapting, changing, or re-prioritizing things to reach your goals.

Update and highlight the skills that support your new focus.

Your certifications, courses, volunteering, and projects can have a big impact on perceptions as you pivot. Use the relevant profile sections to describe what you are learning and doing, but also place the final bow on your profile by using your About description, headline, banner, and Featured section.

> **Sandra's Sidebar**: I used LinkedIn in exactly this way when I left my corporate sales leadership job and started my own LinkedIn consulting business. In my About section I explained how I was an early adopter of LinkedIn and enjoyed helping colleagues use LinkedIn over the years. I wanted to share my journey and in doing so felt that people accepted my new role better.

Action Steps:

- ✓ Assess yourself and decide how to reorient your profile to best tell your story about your pivot.

- ✓ Update your About and headline, as well as any relevant profile sections.
- ✓ Check out the remaining tips in this book and apply them with the lens of your pivot.

Tip #7

Multi-Faceted Professional

If you operate with a "portfolio career" or a side gig, it's important to organize the content of your About essay and Experience section to create as much clarity as possible about you and your brand.

I can't tell you how many people have completely confusing LinkedIn profiles. And no, you can't have two profiles, according to LinkedIn's terms of service. It's our job to make the one excellent profile work for us and appeal to all our various viewers.

Add **multiple** current work experiences to correspond with your professional life now. Each experience should have comprehensive descriptions, titles, geography, skills, and no end date. These may or may not correspond with the same company and that's OK.

Action Steps:

- ✓ Create clear, interesting experience sections for each of your current roles.
- ✓ Update your About essay and headline to tie it all together so that your profile reader is not confused.

You can do it, I promise. This clarity will yield tremendous benefits for your portfolio businesses.

Tip #8

Open to Work: Active or Passive?

LinkedIn provides you the opportunity to share that you are open to a new work opportunity. This feature applies to both active and passive candidates.

Active candidates are usually not working in a current company position. Maybe you were laid off. Some of you may decide to add the Open to Work frame to your profile, but it is a preference. Someone in your network may help connect you to an opportunity if they see your profile frame. If you wish to remain more low-key, you can still activate this feature to display only to recruiters.

Passive candidates usually want to be considered for new opportunities, but wish to keep that under wraps from their current employer. They can also activate the Open to Work feature and only share with recruiters. (LinkedIn claims that the information will not be visible to recruiters at your company, but if you are very concerned about this happening, then don't activate the feature at all.)

For all LinkedIn members using the Open to Work feature, there are other preference settings to be leveraged. Be sure to optimize so you are more likely to be found. If you haven't looked at this in a while, you might wish to update your preferences. You will find the Open to Work feature in your upper Intro Card section.

Action Steps:

- ✓ Decide and then activate the Open to Work feature directly from your Introduction Card (the "Open to" button). Update your preferences.
- ✓ Update your entire profile to articulate to the hiring manager who may view you online. Explain how you bring value to your current or future role.
- ✓ Check out the remaining tips in this book and apply them with the job seeker lens.

Visibility (who can view you're open to work)*

 Recruiters only
Limited to people using LinkedIn Recruiter

While we take steps not to show recruiters at your current company, we can't guarantee complete privacy.

 All LinkedIn members
Includes recruiters and people at your current company

This selection adds the #OpenToWork photo frame.

Tip #9

Hiring Profile

Candidates are looking at your LinkedIn profile if you are a hiring manager or recruiter. Make sure your profile speaks directly to them.

Does your profile...

- clearly show that you are hiring and provide any details for the candidates to get in touch?
- explain the benefits of working on your team?

- describe professional development opportunities at your company?
- focus on values that matter to employees, like work flexibility or diversity?

These are just a few questions, but honestly, I could ask you 50+ such questions. The point is to think broadly about what is important to the candidates you are trying to hire.

Use your About, headline, and Featured sections to describe the opportunities and showcase the company or team. Activate a Hiring frame so that your network knows you are hiring.

Sandra's Sidebar: I love working with hiring manager teams to work on their candidate-friendly profiles. It always makes such a vast difference, so don't delay in making this happen! I also recommend adding candidate-friendly wording to the profiles of your C-suite leaders. Candidates are checking leadership pages too.

Action Steps:

- ✓ Add the Hiring frame.
- ✓ Reorient your profile to speak directly to candidates. If you have additional objectives for your profile, then just weave in the hiring points.

✓ Check out the remaining tips in this book and apply them with the hiring manager lens.

Tip #10

Selling Profile

Many salespeople get things backward for using LinkedIn for sales. They think that their digital engagement, such as messaging and commenting, needs to do the selling work. It's just the opposite.

The profile is what should do the selling for all of us. Use commenting and messaging to build friendly relationships and to get noticed. Once a prospect finds you interesting, they will check out your profile to learn about you and see how you might help them.

In your profile, avoid bragging about beating your sales quota. Instead, focus your About section on how you help your clients achieve their goals. Make sure your skills align with what your prospects and clients value. Look at every aspect of your profile from the lens of your prospect, and then adjust accordingly.

Your expertise needs to shine through, but in a friendly way. You want to come across as a friendly and helpful expert.

> **Sandra's Sidebar**: My company gets hired to work with sales teams all the time. Many of the sales leaders want us to immediately teach how to find prospects, share content, or leverage Sales Navigator. I always pull them back to focus on the profiles first. Always build a great seller profile first, then focus on the engagement opportunities.

Action Steps:

- ✓ Reorient your LinkedIn profile to speak directly to your preferred buyer or prospect.
- ✓ Check out the remaining tips in this book and apply them with the friendly seller lens.

POWERFUL PROSE

Tip #11

Amazing and Proud, Not Boastful

You're amazing. I get it. But don't make the mistake of putting people off by appearing overly boastful.

Why say, "I am the #1 most successful tech salesperson in the US"? If I am a potential buyer, I don't want someone who says they are the best salesperson. I want someone who explains how they can help clients just like me!

Why boast about yourself as a top leader when you have the chance to talk about how proud you are of your team and their development? Do you see the difference here?

Try to avoid superlatives as you describe yourself. Instead, describe your journey, key lessons, or passion for the work. Explain a behind-the-scenes story or your professional story interestingly.

Your incredible accomplishments have their place on LinkedIn. Add your awards to the Honors and Awards section. Display your patents, publications, certifications, etc. in those specific sections. Certainly, do be proud and display your achievements. Just think about how you come across as you describe yourself.

Action Step: As soon as you write the About, Experience, and headline sections, consider the "boastfulness quotient," and decide if you need to change how you describe yourself.

Tip #12

Write in the First Person

LinkedIn is the "professional" social media platform, but you don't want to appear stiff and overly formal!

Avoid writing in the third person. Social media is online conversation and (hopefully) you don't refer to yourself in the third person while talking to people.

Write in the first person using the words "I" or "me." Remember, you are positioning your LinkedIn profile as a conversation starter, not just a place to upload your resume or bio.

> **Sandra's Sidebar:** Save the third-person write-ups for official bios and resumes.

Action Step: Identify which profile sections need to be rewritten. Get help from AI applications if you need help with the editing, but be sure to make it truly your own.

Tip #13

Be Specific

Be clear and specific.

There are millions of "consultants," but certainly not as many wellness, diversity, or legal consultants.

There are millions of salespeople, but not as many with a focus on cyber-security, employee benefits, or marketing automation.

Listing yourself as an attorney on LinkedIn is not helpful. Add the type of law you practice. I may look for a real estate or corporate attorney, and that is what I will search for. Not a general attorney!

There are millions of college seniors every year, but not as many learn about robotics or marketing analytics during a summer internship.

People who are seeking experts with LinkedIn search are looking for very specific expertise. Your prospects don't want generalists.

Action Step: Look at your profile headline, titles, descriptions, and About essay and identify opportunities to be more specific about your expertise. Incorporate your best words into your profile. This is your first step with keywords!

Tip #14

The Magic of Keywords

Keywords are powerful. They help you to be found in search, whether it is Google, YouTube, or LinkedIn. Using vague or out-of-date words in your profile is a mistake that can affect your visibility in search results.

Start by identifying your keywords or key phrases. They should be the words people will use to find someone with your expertise. I recommend nouns and skills primarily for LinkedIn keywords. Stay away from adjectives, adverbs, or articles. Use action verbs sparingly.

Everyone talks about keywords for the search value, and yes, this is huge. But that is not the only benefit. Your carefully selected words affect your brand too. They will create an impression of you and your capabilities when someone views your profile.

Your headline, About essay, Experience, and Skills sections are all valuable places for your keywords.

> **Sandra's Sidebar:** Here is a keyword story for you: I did a LinkedIn Profile workshop for an insurance company's sales team in Hartford, CT a few years ago. This was a deep-dive, hands-on session. Everyone added in their relevant keywords and some of those keywords were unique to their specific markets. One woman in the class specialized in products related to Medicare, so she added that keyword to her profile. Within two weeks, a company in Ohio contacted her specifically looking for that expertise. Keywords can be magic.

Action Steps: Make a list of your keywords and phrases. And be sure to read the next tip about finding keywords just for you. Check out Tip #15 for ideas to help you find keywords.

Tip #15

Unique Ways to Find Keywords, Phrases, and Skills

Are you stuck on identifying keywords, phrases, or skills to match your special capabilities?

Here are some places to help find keywords and skills that you may wish to use on your LinkedIn profile.

- Official job descriptions that appeal to you
- The LinkedIn Skills drop-down list
- Go to the Intro Card of your profile (top of fold). Select "more" and then create a resume. Once you enter the desired job, look for LinkedIn's keyword suggestions.
- Artificial Intelligence prompting; AI apps such as ChatGPT
- LinkedIn page of your company (or ideal company) –check About, Specialties, People, etc.
- Colleague's or competitor's profiles
- LinkedIn's Career Explorer feature
- LinkedIn profiles of influencers in your industry
- LinkedIn content or hashtags
- LinkedIn Groups—research people and topics
- Job board listings
- University alumni pages

Action Step: Use a few ways to help you identify your keywords and skills, but make sure whatever you finally select is a genuine match for your capabilities. (Read tip #14 to learn more about keywords, and tips #23 and #24 to learn more about skills.)

Tip #16

Avoid These Words and Phrases

Try to avoid overused or meaningless words. Some words or phrases just make us look lazy or old. The word *seasoned* comes to mind, along with *demonstrated expertise* as a phrase.

Here's a bad opening statement that I see too often on LinkedIn:

John Smith is a seasoned IT professional with demonstrated expertise in blah, blah. OR, John Smith has a 30-year track record in IT.

UGH.

First, both phrases make John sound old and boring. Unfortunately, very few people seem to care about 30 years of experience or that someone is *seasoned*. These sentences also make John come across as stilted when using the third person.

And finally, why would anyone say that they have demonstrated expertise? Wouldn't you just actually show it, not talk about it?

If this is your opening line in the essay, then I am looking for the door (which means I am going to check out someone else's profile!)

Action Step: Make a note of any phrases or sentences like this and change them ASAP! Also, check out LinkedIn's list of overused words they publish periodically. Google it to get their newest list.

Tip #17

Ready, Set, Action

Use active verbs in your writing on LinkedIn. Passive voice sounds…well, passive, and may make a poor impression on the reader.

Examples of active verbs are:

- Develop
- Build
- Sell
- Manage
- Create
- Teach

Action Step: Take out the word "responsibility" or the phrase "responsible for" and replace it with an active verb and a relevant accomplishment.

Tip #18

Your About Essay—Be Interesting

The About essay is a golden opportunity to introduce yourself memorably and impress your viewer. You want to be interesting!

If your essay is only about you, it's probably not that interesting.

Write a first-person essay and include how you help and the value you bring. And, yes, you can do this without boasting.

Too many essays are regurgitated bios focusing on the past. Consider telling your story and sharing your insights. I know you can make your profile interesting and relevant!

Here is a quick rundown of my special **5H format** for About essays.

- **Hook**: Start with an **interesting** story, fact, or insight (not boasting). The goal is to get your viewer to click "See More" to read the entire essay.
- **Help**: Describe who you help and how you help. This might be a client or employer. This lets them know how you can bring value to your profile reader and their organization.
- **Human**: Tell your reader what you do for fun or share your personal interests. Who you are outside of work is a valuable piece of your personal brand image. Be human!
- **Hot words**: Include your personal keywords or key phrases. List them as specialties or focus areas. These are words that can be used to search for or validate you.
- **Hello**: Be sure to add how you like to be contacted with your contact information, or suggest how best to connect with you. Always make it easy to be contacted.

Action Steps:

- ✓ Tell the right story to attract and impress your perfect client, partner, candidate, or employer. Try the 5H format. Be genuine. Be yourself.
- ✓ Need some examples of the 5H format or some itive prompts? Download this book's **Companion** le.

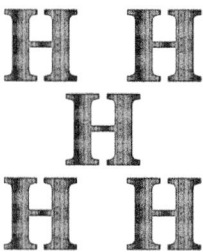

Tip #19

Powerful Headline

Your headline should position you immediately with your ideal profile viewer. Consider it your personal tagline. Your headline doesn't need to be the same as your job title.

You have up to 220 characters now, so consider expanding it to take advantage of the additional real estate. Please also realize that the beginning of the headline is more widely seen by others as you are being found in search or engaging on the platform. People who arrive at your full profile will see all 220 characters.

Make it clear how you help and what value you deliver. Leverage current and strategic keywords in your headline. Consider naming your target audience to add additional clarity.

Consider using keywords, skills, nouns, and verbs in such a way that your profile reader understands your value and how you help them. Don't be too cute or unique. Avoid words like ninja, guru, or genius.

You have some latitude with the formatting. Here are some headline formats:

- Powerful keywords (with separators)
- Value-based mini bio
- Combination of keyword and value-based
- Role or title with keywords and/or value
- Personal brand identity phrase followed by keywords or value provided

Action Steps:

- ✓ Start writing various headline possibilities for yourself. Write several.
- ✓ Download the **Companion Guide** to see headline examples corresponding to each format.
- ✓ Finalize your headline selection and enter it into your profile.

> **Sandra's Sidebar:** Your photo and headline are the two most important parts of your LinkedIn profile. This is what viewers will see first when you are engaged on the platform.

Tip #20

Multilingual Capabilities

Do you want to take your additional language(s) capabilities a step further? Are you multilingual? I think speaking multiple languages is very impressive and could absolutely help you attract new business or career opportunities.

Besides the regular language profile section, you have the option to add a second language profile that is connected to your main (English) version.

You will need to provide your own translation for the About, headline, Experience, and Education sections. You can do this yourself or get some help from an Artificial Intelligence tool.

Make yourself visible more broadly by adding a second language profile!

Action Step: Translate your About, headline, Experience, and Education. Create a new second language profile. This task is easier than ever with help from Artificial Intelligence.

MORE PROFILE SECTIONS

Tip #21

Work Experience

Your work experience section is extremely valuable and contributes to search optimization and your brand image.

Select a company name from the drop-down menu to display your employer's logo. Always include your title, dates, location, skills, and description. Select from drop-down menus.

Use keywords or phrases naturally in the description. Write your Experience section in the first person. Optionally include media and type of position.

Strong work experience descriptions are essential for your successful profile. Emphasize the growth, evolution, or key value deliverables for each position. Highlight relevant transferrable skills that are important for your current situation or goals.

You can write your description in paragraph or bullet list format. Or you can write a short paragraph description followed by the bullet points. Whenever possible, list your accomplishments with active verbs and specific data or impact such as "increased sales YOY in 2023 by 17%." Relevant metrics are especially important for job seekers. Recruiters are looking for statistics.

If you are a business development person, consider adding the success metrics for your clients instead of your own. Use the description section to write about who you serve, the geography you cover, your services or products, and how you help clients.

> **Sandra's Sidebar**: The Experience and Education sections are what I like to call the "meat and potatoes" of a LinkedIn profile. The most interested viewers will scroll down to look at these sections more closely. Make them sing!

Action Step: Write or update your current Experience section now. Be sure to include the description part and make it friendly by writing in the first person.

Tip #22

Career Break or Not Currently Working?

There seems to be less of a stigma for taking a career break than there was years ago. Thank goodness!

You now have the option of adding an official Career Break to your experience section. This is completely optional and based on preference. Your choices in the LinkedIn profile currently include Bereavement, Career Transition, Caregiving, Full-time Parenting, Gap Year, Layoff, Health and Wellbeing, Personal Goal Pursuit, Professional Development, Relocation, Retirement, Travel, and Voluntary Work.

If this situation applies to you, simply add the Career Break section to your profile and fill out the entries. Find this in the "Add a Profile" section. Be sure to add a description and tell your story.

There's another option for those in transition. If you are not working now and actively searching for a new position, consider adding a new current work experience section to your profile. You will need to give yourself a title and include dates, location, skills, and a description. Consider what you are doing now and how best to display it. Are you consulting, studying, or pivoting? You can call yourself a consultant or student if this fits you.

Within the current experience section, you can also give yourself the title of the new job you are seeking and then describe how you are working toward that goal. Be honest and make clear your intentions so there is no misunderstanding of your role. Doing this will make you more findable in search for that specific role.

> **Sandra's Sidebar**: Most people find that sharing their Career Break online is a good conversation starter. It lets people learn about your values. Other LinkedIn users decide to keep this information private. You decide what is best for you.

Action Step: Add a Career Break or a new current experience section to your profile, if applicable and helpful to you.

Tip #23

Add and Accentuate Skills

Select the skills that you possess and wish to highlight on your profile. Be sure to incorporate relevant keywords that describe your expertise. Avoid adjectives and adverbs. Instead, pick skills related to the major LinkedIn categories. Select from the drop-down menus.

LinkedIn's Skills categories include:

- Industry knowledge
- Tools and technologies
- Interpersonal skills

You have the option to add up to 100 skills now to the main Skills section, but the top 2 are the most visible on your profile. Select your relevant skills and then position the most strategic ones into those top spots.

Your skills are in the Skills section in the main body of your profile. However, now you can also add skills to several other parts of your profile, such as About, Education, and Experience. This is an excellent improvement in LinkedIn profiles. Be sure to do this!

Skills are important because they can be used in the LinkedIn search to find you. They help to create an impression of you and your capabilities. They are also a factor in LinkedIn's collaborative articles.

Action Steps:

- ✓ Add up to 100 skills in the main Skills section. Use the drop-down menu.

ritize your two most important skills for your career now and rearrange them on top.

Download the **Companion Guide** to see a video demonstration of how to do this.

Tip #24

Endorsements

Validate and showcase the Skills on your LinkedIn profile with some third-party social proof of your capabilities.

Your connections can endorse you for your skills. This is an excellent idea! You can ask your clients and colleagues to endorse you with a simple click on your skill. Be sure to endorse other people too. Of course, do this authentically when each person is aware and witness to the other person's genuine skills.

> **Sandra's Sidebar:** Skill Endorsements had a bumpy start as a LinkedIn feature over 10 years ago. I like this feature when used properly. Give and get endorsements as a friendly pat on the back with your connections. It's OK to suggest to a colleague that you work well with and say "let's endorse each other for skills we possess." I think your coworker will be pleased to take part.

Action Steps:

- ✓ Ask your colleague or client to endorse you at the appropriate time.

✓ Generously endorse other people authentically for their skills.

Tip #25

Your Learning Brand

Employers, partners, clients, and candidates all love to be associated with learners.

Add your higher and secondary education institutions to the Education section. Don't worry if you don't yet have a degree. Once you receive your degree (if ever) you can add it to your profile at that time.

If you have multiple colleges, consider including them all in your profile for optimal networking.

Feature your most relevant education entry in your Introduction Card at the top of your profile. You do this by positioning your most important education entry to the top of the Education field.

I also recommend adding your high school to the Education section! This is a nice networking conversation starter.

For each Education entry, include your school's name, location, major, and completed degrees. Use the drop-down selections whenever possible. The attendance and graduation dates are optional but recommended for most people.

Don't forget to include a description next to each school. Use that to share your most relevant activities and interests. This contributes to the personalization of your profile.

For professional development courses, continuing education, certifications, and leadership programs, add those to either the Course or Certification sections of your profile. Talk about your strategic learning journey in your About section, too.

Action Steps:

- ✓ Add or update your Education, Courses, and Certifications sections.
- ✓ Download the **Companion Guide** to view the video on editing Education, including hiding dates and moving your most relevant education section to the top of your profile.

Tip #26

Leverage the Services Page

If you are a freelancer or service provider, don't miss out on the wonderful opportunity of creating a Services page that is connected to your personal profile. The Services page gives you much greater visibility in search. People may be looking for your services.

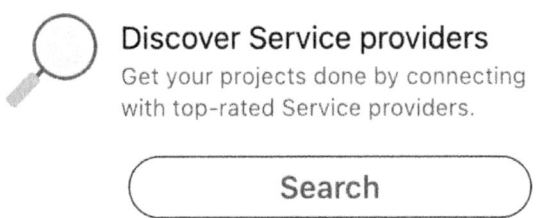

Why not take advantage of the opportunity to showcase your services?

Enter your location and list of services and fill in all the relevant subsections of the Services page. Optimize the About description and use close to the 500 characters allowed to describe your services. Consider adding media to showcase your work here as well, which is currently available to premium users.

Set up your page and ask a few clients to write a review for your page. This adds to your online credibility.

Be sure to activate this feature if you are a freelancer or service provider because it will enhance the ability of your freelance prospects to find you on LinkedIn.

Action Step: Add or update your Services page if applicable to you. Do it today. (This feature is currently available by going to the Add Profile Section tab from your Introduction Card.)

Tip #27

Be Easy to Contact

Yes, some people will message you directly on LinkedIn. Others will be looking for your contact information because they wish to go offline and have a conversation.

I recommend you add your email and work phone number in multiple places on your profile, so you are easy to contact.

Besides the official Contact Info section found in the Introduction Card, be sure to include your contact information and call to action in your About section if you are comfortable doing so. Invite your profile viewers into conversation or suggest a next step. By the way, this is the final **H** (Hello) in my **5H** format for the About section.

If you are concerned about your privacy, you can hide it and invite your viewers to use LinkedIn messaging to reach you. This is easier for those with an Open Profile activated from their premium accounts. (Open Profile has settings so you can allow inbound messages from people you aren't connected to)

I use LinkedIn to find people I wish to work with or refer. Half the time, their profile doesn't include any contact information. I just move on. It's so easy to avoid this mistake.

Don't let this be you. Instead, be easy to contact.

> **Sandra's Sidebar**: You also need to decide about which phone number to add. I wouldn't enter a home number or address and I suggest including work contact information only for most people.

Action Step: Consider adding or updating your contact information in the Contact Info section *and* at the bottom of your About essay.

Tip #28

Credibility-Boosting Sections

LinkedIn offers many additional sections which may apply to you now or in the future. Go to "Add a Profile Section" to add them. These entries will certainly add to your credibility.

Do any of these apply to you?

- Publications
- Organizations
- Volunteering
- Languages
- Honors and Awards
- Certifications
- Patents
- Projects

If so, enter the specific details along with a description and links when applicable. Always use drop-down menus as you make your selections.

Interestingly, the Certifications and Volunteering sections have a priority position within the profile. They are currently above the Skills section. LinkedIn made this position change over the last few years.

Action Step: Add or update all the special sections that apply to you.

VISUAL VITALITY

Tip #29

Smile

Your LinkedIn profile should convey that you are friendly and approachable. If you don't have a photo or you aren't smiling, you're making a mistake. Your profile viewers will decide if you are friendly or trustworthy, largely based on your picture.

Choose an image that represents you well. Avoid using selfies or picture cut-outs. Make your headshot image of your head and shoulders, not a full-body shot. Be sure to crop your picture so that your face is very visible when viewed from a mobile app.

When you upload the picture to LinkedIn, double-check your settings to make sure the public and everyone can see your photo. The default setting is viewable for **Public/Anyone/Everyone**, and is not limited to your connections. Unfortunately, I have uncovered many clients who had previously changed the setting and were unaware that new contacts couldn't view their picture. It's always best to double-check your settings.

If you want to get some impartial feedback, ask a friend, or upload your photo to www.photofeeler.com

Sandra's Sidebar: Not too long ago, I advised clients to wear a suit and tie for photos, but that is no longer the case. You decide what you want to wear based on your profession. Things are more relaxed now. Some people even use AI to help them with their headshots. It's an option for an inexpensive solution, but I recommend uploading an actual photo of you.

Action Steps: Upload your photo to LinkedIn and check your photo visibility settings. Some people inadvertently keep the profile visible only to connections, so new people you meet with not see your photo! (See link to settings in the Companion Guide.)

Tip #30

Background Photo (Banner) Ideas

Consider which background photo will best represent your brand image or expertise. You can pick a favorite photo or create an image. Think about how the banner will coincide with your About, headline, and the rest of your profile to create one cohesive brand look and impression.

Background banners are partially obstructed by your headshot, so plan accordingly. Some older banners look pretty bad now because a few years ago, LinkedIn changed the headshot position. Do you need to update yours?

A Few Ideas For Background Photos:

- A custom image that motivates and inspires your ideal profile viewer. What could that be for you?
- An image that represents your functional or industry expertise
- Image of you at work or with your team
- Word cloud representing your profession or skills
- Image related to your career story or professional journey
- Image of your book or special certification
- An image that shows your values
- Photo from your town, city, or harbor

LinkedIn offers images to choose from if you are stuck. Those will probably keep improving. Many people use Canva to help them easily create a background photo. You can also create using Artificial Intelligence tools such as Dall-E or Microsoft Designer.

Sandra's Sidebar: Consider updating your background photo regularly. Keep it fresh and relevant to what is current and exciting in your professional life. Think about what you wish to communicate about yourself now. Consider your ideal viewer and what will appeal to them.

Action Steps: Pick a concept that aligns with your brand. Create or source a new banner. Download the **Companion Guide** for this book to see a few examples. Double-check that your banner looks good on the mobile app, too.

Tip #31

Sourcing Images the Right Way

You may wish to create your own background banner and need to find images. Or you wish to add images to other parts of your profile.

Be sure to acquire images the safe way. This means only displaying images on LinkedIn with proper permission. Don't just grab an image from Google and call it a day. Here are the best options:

- Photos you have taken yourself
- Images or banners that you have designed in Canva or another tool
- Pictures or banners that you have ordered from Fiverr.com or elsewhere
- Photos that you own or have purchased

- Royalty-free images that are marked "Available for commercial use" and "Attribution free." Check out Pexels.com and Pixabay.com for options.
- Consider AI-generated images, but be cautious because these are so new, and the AI legal landscape is changing rapidly.

Action Step: Create, source, or select your images or background banners. Upload to your profile.

Tip #32

Sizzling Multimedia Profile

Use a sizzling multimedia portfolio approach for your LinkedIn profile. This will make your profile more engaging and showcase your capabilities. The optimal location for media display is in the Featured section. Remember to keep your media up to date. Consider including:

- Videos
- Documents
- Website landing pages
- Calendar links
- Blog posts or articles
- Top LinkedIn posts

Your viewers will gain a sense of how you work and your thought leadership expertise.

The media on the far left is the most important and will be the only one displayed on the mobile app.

Sandra's Sidebar: LinkedIn introduced the Featured section during the early part of the COVID-19 pandemic. This is my favorite profile feature. Use this to highlight your professional portfolio.

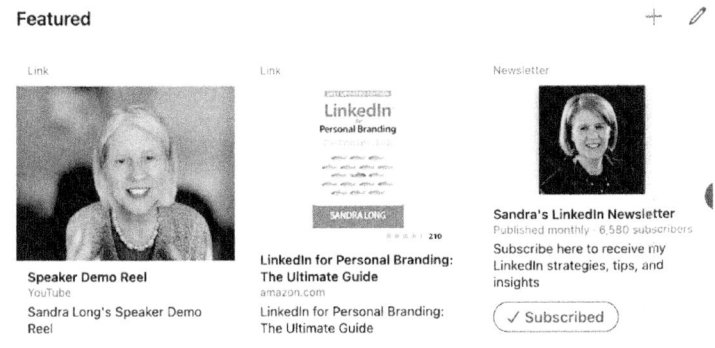

Action Steps:

- ✓ Inventory your personal media assets.
- ✓ Upload relevant media or links to the Featured section.
- ✓ Prioritize and arrange your most strategic entries to appear first on your profile.

Tip #33

Leverage Additional Media

My favorite place to display media on LinkedIn is the Featured section. However, here is a list of the other parts of the profile where you can display your media, such as images, videos, or documents:

- Experience section
- Education section
- Licenses and Certifications
- Services page

Pick the right media that coincides with the various sections and keep the most strategic ones above in the Featured section.

> **Sandra's Sidebar:** I display media from my educational institutions and work positions on my profile as well as several others. It adds depth to your entries. Consider this idea for yourself.

Action Step: Look through your entire profile and make a list of the sections where you plan to add media. Now, make it happen!

Tip #34

White Space

White space is your friend!

Massive paragraphs with no breaks or bullets will stop your readers in their tracks. Nobody wants to read them.

Create white space by writing short snappy paragraphs.

Consider using bullets or icons to create lists, if appropriate.

Always strive for a nice clean look for your text. White space is key!

> **Sandra's Sidebar**: When I see a long running paragraph, I run for the hills. It surprises me how many people add them to their LinkedIn profiles. But I know you won't make that mistake!

Action Step: Review your entire profile to make sure it has a nice, clean appearance.

Tip #35

Emojis or No?

It's a funny 😜 thing about emojis. Some people love them, and others clearly do not. My opinion has changed since the COVID-19 pandemic, and I am not sure why. I think it's because I just feel more relaxed about everything.

Emoji use and acceptance are growing rapidly among all age groups. The countries with the most emoji adoption include Japan, the United States, and Brazil.

I do recommend using emojis sparingly in the About and Experience sections, as well as in your content. Because of the debate on this issue, I researched the value of emojis for the name or headline fields using ChatGPT. My suspicion was confirmed. Search algorithms prioritize text, so it makes sense to be cautious about using them in headlines.

Whatever you decide on emojis, don't overdo it. Use them sparingly to add some visual spice and color. Consider deploying them to lighten up your profile in the About section and throughout the profile in the description areas.

Action Step: Add a few relevant and tasteful emojis in your About and Experience sections. Don't go overboard.

Tip #36

Create a Custom Presentation

Are you trying to get selected, hired, or referred? Whether you are a job seeker or a business builder, I know you may want to be found and advance your professional goals, because you decided to spend time on LinkedIn.

Your LinkedIn profile is a wonderful representation of your brand. It is a place to demonstrate your portfolio. And there is so much more opportunity.

Why not go a step further and create a custom presentation just for your LinkedIn profile?

Think about your ideal profile visitor. Is it a client, prospect, or a hiring manager?

What can you share to motivate them to connect with, message, or hire you?

Create a custom video or PowerPoint explaining your approach, vision, or the special ways you work.

Answer a burning question in your presentation, such as one of these:

- "Why should I hire you?"
- "Here's what to expect if you work with me."
- "Why did clients hire me?"
- "Why is my company unique?"
- "The top 7 industry trends and how they will affect you."

Action Step: Create and upload your custom presentation into the Featured Section of your profile.

MORE WAYS TO BE FOUND

Tip #37

Complete Your Profile

Did you know LinkedIn will display your profile in a search result more often if your profile is complete? What are you missing out on?

Your LinkedIn profile is much more than your online resume. Be thorough and complete all relevant sections.

Optimize your profile with current and accurate information, including your work experience, education, skills, About essay, volunteering, and more. Click on "Add Profile Section" to check out all the options of sections to add.

Be sure to write in the description fields. Consider writing in brief paragraphs or include bullet points.

Some people don't know what to say or how to say it, so they say nothing. But that's just giving up on opportunities, because any viewers you have will turn elsewhere. Similarly, if your content is out of date, displaying old skills or certifications, your viewers won't know what you offer.

Finally, LinkedIn is less likely to display an incomplete profile. Ouch!

Action Step: Complete all sections today so you will be more easily found.

Tip #38

Use the Name Field Properly

You must enter your name properly in your profile, so you are easily found and are following LinkedIn's terms of service.

Your name field is intended for your name only. The only exception is you may add professional designations such as CPA, CSP, MBA, PhD, or CFP.

Don't add keywords, phone numbers, or website addresses. I often see people who include a keyword-rich headline inside their name field. LinkedIn prohibits this usage; and it also makes your profile look amateurish. It also makes it awkward for people to mention you effectively.

Here's what works and doesn't work:

Jeremy Jones ✓

Jennifer Jones, CPA ✓

Jason Jones, Marketing Consultant

P.S. Consider adding a former or maiden name which will appear like this:

Jenna (Smith) Jones

> **Sandra's Sidebar:** Take the name field advice seriously. You want your name to be clearly visible and easy to @mention. You want to follow the LinkedIn terms of service, too. When I teach corporate groups, oftentimes 20-30% of attendees need to change their names for some reason.

Action Step: Adjust your name if needed.

Tip #39

Customize Your URL

Customize your LinkedIn URL for these three benefits:

- Make it easier for people to find you.
- You will appear as a savvier user.
- The cleaner URL will be more attractive for your resume or bio.

Do this by clicking on "Edit public profile & URL" on your profile page, which is currently in the upper right corner. I recommend removing all the numerical digits and trying to select a URL that is close to your actual name.

If you can't get the URL you want, LinkedIn will offer alternative suggestions. Ideally, you can try to get your first and last name. You may have to get your last name first or add a middle initial, since there are now so many LinkedIn users.

Old URL Example

www.linkedin.com/in/jenniferjones-14578

New URL Example (with middle initial Z)

www.linkedin.com/in/jenniferzjones

Action Step: Customize your URL and try to claim your name. Clear out those numeric digits.

Tip #40

Optimize Your Location

Be sure to add your location to your profile. Find this in the "Edit Intro" section. Your location will appear on your Introduction Card of your profile.

You will enter your postal code first. Then LinkedIn gives you the option of selecting one of two choices for the city and state.

For example, my postal code of 03833 prompts me to select either Exeter, New Hampshire, or Greater Boston. If you are like me and focused on finding clients and opportunities, then consider picking the major city. My Introduction Card features "Greater Boston," not my little New Hampshire town.

If you are planning on moving somewhere and want to be found in that future location, select the new city. This is especially helpful for job seekers or graduating seniors who are relocating. Be sure to explain in your About section that you are planning to relocate to ease any confusion.

> **Sandra's Sidebar**: Besides the main location field in the upper fold (Introduction Card) consider the location names listed for each experience section. These fields allow more flexibility.

Action Step: Check and adjust your location in the Introduction Card editing section. Also, review and adjust locations related to your experiences.

Tip #41

Select Your Industry

Select your industry in the Edit Intro section.

Choose from the drop-down menu. People complain about the choices, which were expanded recently. Just select the closest one to your industry.

Chances are you have an old industry loaded inside your profile, so now's the best time to update it.

Even though the industry is not that visible, it is a search filter so you want it to be accurate and up-to-date so the right people can find you.

> **Sandra's Sidebar**: Some students in my profile class struggle to pick the right industry. Sometimes you have a few that may apply. For example, if you are an HR professional working at a marketing company, which do you select? Well, that is up to you and should tie in with your goals. So, if you wish to get a new job in HR and don't care about marketing, then select HR. If you are more interested in staying in the marketing industry, then select marketing.

Action Step: Review the newest industry options and update your industry selection accordingly.

Tip #42

Use Drop-Down Menus

Throughout your LinkedIn profile, there are sections where you may either choose a drop-down option or add your own words.

Always try to use one of LinkedIn's standard word choices from their drop-down menus whenever possible. The LinkedIn search filters rely on those standard inputs first. You want your profile to be more easily found within the LinkedIn database.

Here are some examples of how to use the drop-down menus on LinkedIn:

- In the Experience section, select your employer's name from the drop-down to see the logo on your profile. Select a standard title from the menu whenever possible.
- In the Skills section, try to select pre-populated skills from the list.
- In the Education section, select the university name from the drop-down menu to view the logo on your profile. Try to select the degree name from the LinkedIn list, too.
- In the Licenses and Certifications section, try to pick from the drop-down choices.

Action Step: Do a quick check of your profile. Look for missing logos and replace the names with a selection from the drop-down menu.

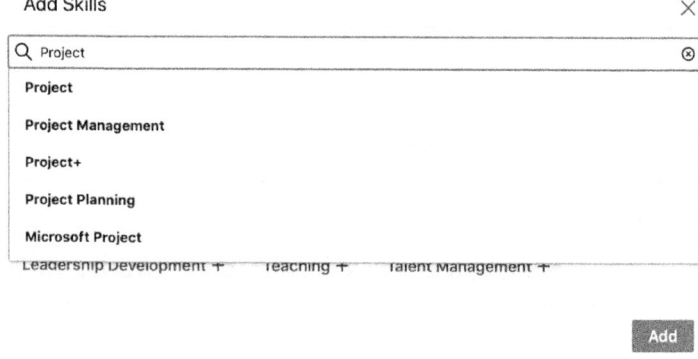

Tip #43

Be Found via Google

Besides being found via LinkedIn, you want to be found by your new prospect who enters your name in Google or Bing. You want the LinkedIn profile to be optimized and visible everywhere because this should be your best foot forward online.

LinkedIn calls this your "Public Profile."

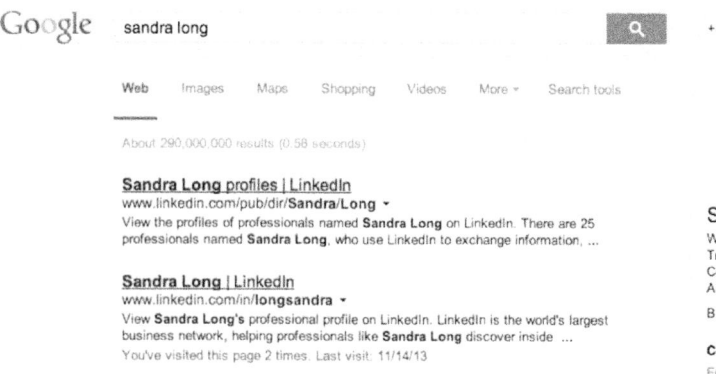

LinkedIn gives you many options of what you can display publicly. I highly recommend making your entire profile and photo visible publicly. This is a wonderful opportunity to be seen professionally!

> **Sandra's Sidebar:** Google and other search engines love LinkedIn profiles. This is an immense advantage. Just make sure you are set up to be found by following this advice.

Action Steps:

- ✓ Update your public profile settings by going to the Settings and Privacy section or look at the upper right corner of your profile and select "Edit Public Profile."
- ✓ Google yourself periodically.

Tip #44

Be Found via Your Network

Your ability to be found in search also depends on your LinkedIn network.

Try to have at least 500 first-level connections. These should be people you know or have a logical connection with. For example, your network should include your current and past coworkers, clients, prospects, fellow students or alumni, neighbors, industry partners, community connections, friends, and relatives.

Even as a new user or college student, it makes sense to strive for at least 500 meaningful connections. Consider all the college and high school friends you can invite. Your network can grow fast. Aim for quality over quantity, of course.

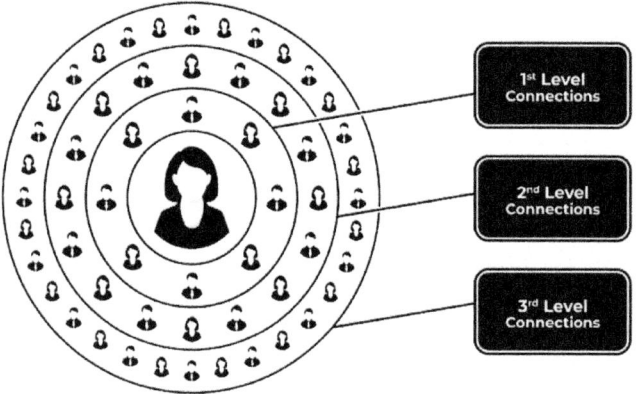

Sandra's Sidebar: Many of my new clients immediately ask to go hunting for prospects. Yes, I love to show them how to do this. However, it will be much easier to find valuable new connections if you have systematically connected with your professional network already. Take the time and connect with all the folks you know and trust first.

Action Step: Systematically add meaningful LinkedIn connections. First, connect with your backlog based on your network. Second, do this routinely every day to coincide with your professional journey.

SWEET SPOTS

Tip #45

Recommendations

Why not let others brag about you? There is no need for you to do this yourself. Conversely, be the one to recommend others generously.

LinkedIn Recommendations are the best type of social proof. These written testimonials will be displayed on your profile and on the profile of the recommender. Wow!

I recommend asking your boss, coworkers, mentors, partners, colleagues, employers, and clients for recommendations for your profile. These recommendations add credibility and showcase your capabilities.

How to do this? Always start with a conversation first and then send over the link from your LinkedIn account. Follow up if you need to do so.

Here's a secret: The people who have the most LinkedIn Recommendations are the ones who *ask* for them.

I recommend creating a habit. Figure out the triggers in your business or career that should prompt you to seek a recommendation. Possible recommendation triggers include:

- Project completion—can you ask your customer, coworker, or manager?

- Promotion—ask your manager and coworkers
- Switching jobs—ask your customer(s), manager, or coworkers
- Customer compliment—ask for a recommendation right away!
- Add your triggers to this list!

⚡ Newsflash: Giving recommendations is just as important—maybe even more important—than receiving them. Let's face it—the top leaders are generous recommenders.

Always be authentic. You are only recommending people who are very talented and deserve a testimonial from you. It should never be fake.

> **Sandra's Sidebar**: It's OK to ask a colleague if you can recommend each other. So why not give some thought to all those successful team projects and plan to write and receive recommendations?

Action Steps:

- ✓ Give three surprise LinkedIn Recommendations to your connections today. Enjoy their reaction!
- ✓ Have a conversation with a coworker, client, or partner about recommending each other. Do this today too.

Tip #46

Activity Spotlight

You can now decide which of your LinkedIn content to display most prominently on your profile. I recommend looking at this periodically.

For example, if you are someone who comments but never posts, then switch the display so your comments are visible to profile visitors.

This is a great opportunity to showcase your preferred content. The current choices are:

- Posts
- Comments
- Videos
- Images
- Newsletters
- Events
- Documents

> **Sandra's Sidebar**: This is one of my favorite new profile tips. Super quick and extremely powerful.

Action Step: Check this feature now and decide what you will display.

What content do you want to show first?

Your recent activity will only display content from the past 360 days.

- ● Posts
- ○ Comments
- ○ Videos
- ○ Images
- ○ Articles
- ○ Newsletter
- ○ Events (None posted in the past year)
- ○ Documents (None posted in the past year)

Tip #47

Distinguish Yourself as a Thought Leader

Pick your core thought leadership themes or topics. Select topics that will attract your ideal customer and that epitomize your expertise and interests.

Raise your visibility by commenting on LinkedIn with valuable insights. Commenting is the #1 thing you can do! Follow the 80% rule and comment more often than posting. Yes, I said that correctly. Focus your efforts on commenting.

Your comments should be valuable insights or an interesting way to extend the conversation. Find content that applies to you, your brand, and your expertise. There will be people who will notice you and reach out to you. A new connection asked me to speak on their podcast after he read my comments about using LinkedIn to drive success with an event.

And now, LinkedIn is awarding *Top Voice Community Badges* for profiles of users who actively contribute to their AI-fueled Collaborative Articles. LinkedIn is reporting a significant increase in views of your contributions, and they are seen via Google. The company is offering a nice little profile bonus with these badges. However, the ability to engage in various topics is more important to me. I enjoy adding my two cents to subjects where I have expertise to share.

Here's what you do. Review the topics and select those to match your capabilities. Be sure that the skills in your About section also match your chosen article entries. Click through to see the paragraphs and prompts.

> **Sandra's Sidebar**: If you only have time for one thought leadership activity I recommend strategically commenting on other people's posts.

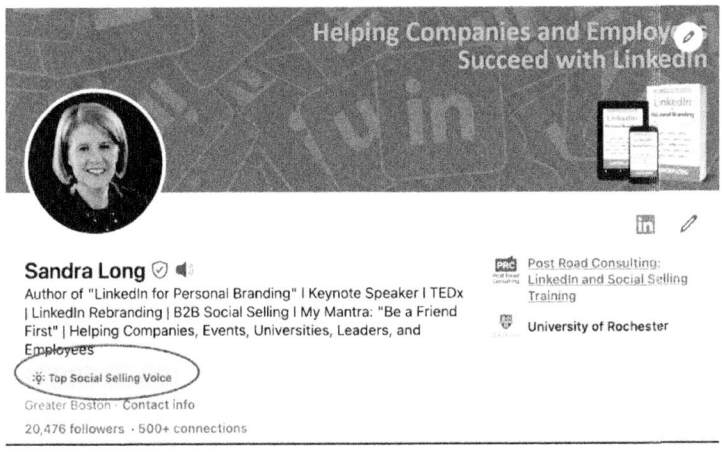

Action Steps:

- ✓ Decide if you will focus on commenting, collaborating, or both. Incorporate your unique insights and stories.
- ✓ Download the companion guide to this book for the link to Collaborative Articles. Find the link and add your insights to an article. You can do this today.
- ✓ Read my *LinkedIn for Personal Branding* book for more comprehensive advice about content and thought leadership using LinkedIn.

Tip #48

Drive Website Traffic

Website traffic today comes from LinkedIn, Facebook, X (formerly Twitter), Instagram, YouTube, Snapchat, and TikTok. For business or career-minded people, LinkedIn is your best source of traffic.

LinkedIn drives traffic to websites every day. What about yours?

Make sure you have capitalized on all the opportunities in your profile to add relevant URLs and website links:

- Include 3 of your website links (or key URLs) in the Contact Info section
- Multiple links can go in the Featured Section. Pick those that create a nice visual appearance and link to good content.

- Include blog articles in your Publications section.
- Add webpages to your Project pages. Be sure to write up a nice description to accompany the link.
- Add a link to your top Introduction Card as a premium user (Custom button).
- Add links to media under Experience, Education, Volunteering, and Awards
- Link to any credential URL from the Licenses and Certifications section
- Add the patent URL from the Patents section

Sandra's Sidebar: Besides the profile links, you can drive traffic to your website from your LinkedIn company page, events, and content.

Action Step: Do an audit of your profile to make sure you have optimized your URL linking opportunities.

Tip #49

Add Audio Name Pronunciation

Is your name difficult to pronounce? Make it easy for people to greet you.

Create a 10-second audio recording of your name along with a quick greeting. Record this in the LinkedIn mobile app, but listen to it on either platform.

You are doing your profile visitor a favor by sharing the correct pronunciation of your name.

> **Sandra's Sidebar:** Even if your name is easy to pronounce consider recording your name for your profile visitors. It's nice for people to hear your voice.

Action Step: Record your name pronunciation greeting on the mobile app today.

Tip #50

Add Gender Pronouns

Select your gender pronouns if you wish to display them next to your name field. This is an important feature for many LinkedIn users. For some people, gender pronouns are an important part of their brand identity. For others, they wish to communicate that they are an ally.

You may select:

She/Her
He/Him
They/Them

Or enter a custom pronoun.

Action Step: Decide if you wish to include gender pronouns in your profile. If yes, enter them in the "Edit Intro" section.

TECHNICAL FOUNDATIONS

Tip #51

Profile Editing

Make most of your profile edits on your desktop or laptop.

The mobile app is not the best place to change your profile. However, the app is the only place where you can record your name pronunciation.

To make profile edits on your computer, look for:

- Pencil icon (✎) to edit
- Plus sign (+) to add
- Trash sign (🗑) to delete
- "Add Profile Section" to add new sections.
- The "Edit" pencil icon in the Introduction Card to make updates to your name, location, industry, headline, gender, and more.

This is just a partial list of how to make profile edits!

> **Sandra's Sidebar**: There are a few tricky editing hacks, so be sure to watch the video I created for readers.

Action Step: Download the **Companion Guide** and watch the profile editing video which shows you how to make all the edits.

Tip #52

Broadcast Your Profile Updates?

Decide if you wish to announce your profile changes to your network. This really is your choice.

If you are adding in an exciting new position, you may wish to enable this feature. You can expect to get a lot of attention when you push out the announcement of a new job or promotion.

Conversely, if you are cleaning up your profile and adding older roles, it may be best to turn this announcement feature to the *off* position. Another situation when it makes sense to turn it off is if you are working to make your profile complete and adding a lot of items at once.

The feature is called "Share Profile Edits." Find it in the Settings and Privacy part of your LinkedIn account.

Action Step: Decide whether you wish to broadcast changes and update the settings in Settings and Privacy accordingly.

Tip #53

Download and Learn the Mobile App

It comes in handy to look up potential clients before you meet in person in a coffee shop. You don't want to be without the app. Can you imagine the horrors? (Yes, this is how I think!)

Always be ready to meet and greet and use LinkedIn to help you!

Activate the "app only" features from the mobile app. For example, you can use it to enter your 10-second name pronunciation or to send an audio or video message.

> **Sandra's Sidebar**: The benefits of using the LinkedIn mobile app include convenient networking, job searching, and accessing professional content on the go. I always double-check a contact's profile before meeting at Dunkin' or Starbucks. This quick last-minute research step improves every conversation!

Action Step: Download the mobile app right now! Log in and get familiar with the navigation. Add your name pronunciation if you haven't already done so or consider sending a friendly audio or video message.

Tip #54

Leverage the Profile QR Code

QR (Quick Response) code popularity is surging globally, according to everything I read and of course by my first-hand witness. Now, most smartphone cameras recognize QR codes, so this increases ease of use and adoption.

A QR code stores information, which is quickly scanned and read by smartphones. We are seeing them pop up everywhere. This easy shortcut provides easy access to websites, landing pages, or links. You will save time and impress your network if you use this LinkedIn feature.

QR codes are a wonderful resource. And the LinkedIn profile QR code is fantastic! Now you can share it with a new contact to make an instant connection.

Find your QR code right from the mobile app. Press on the small QR code icon while you are in the My Network section of the app. You can use this to share with a new contact for an immediate connection. Or grab a phone screenshot to use in a presentation or display on your business card.

Sandra's Sidebar: This is an amazing feature for all your events! Use it to supercharge your connecting. However, don't get lazy. Follow up with your new connections by sending a friendly note.

Action Step: Look for your profile QR code right now. Currently, find it in the My Network tab in your mobile app. Find it lower right side of the app. Click on the plus sign. Other users will find it by clicking on the upper search bar.

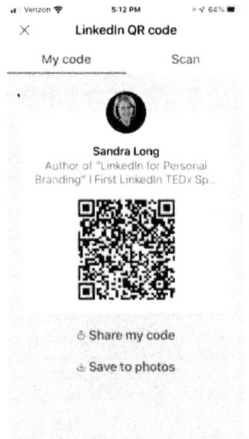

Tip #55

Profile Visibility Settings

LinkedIn is constantly updating its settings options. Therefore, it is a smart idea to check the Settings and Privacy section in your LinkedIn account regularly.

You will find most of the settings related to your profile under the two sub-headings:

- Account Preferences
- Visibility

I believe that being open and visible is the right strategy for most of us. Be sure to show your last name and photo, for example.

> **Sandra's Sidebar**: I always suggest keeping your network visible and open for connections to view. This shows you are ready to make connections and introduce others. Being open to networking embodies the true spirit of LinkedIn. Also, I want people to see that I have viewed their profile. Think of it this way. It is not "stalking," but a genuine compliment to view someone's profile. It shows interest.

Action Step: Review and decide on all your LinkedIn settings.

Tip #56

Email Considerations

This tip seems so simple, but please follow my advice here to avoid a lot of future aggravation. Protect yourself and your account with this tip!

Enter all of your email addresses into your LinkedIn account. You select the primary email, which displays at the top of your profile in the Introduction Card. Do this in the Settings and Privacy area of your page.

Here are two reasons to include all of them:

- Avoid the chance of you mistakenly setting up a duplicate account.
- Avoid being shut out if your email has a problem or you change companies.

Action Step: Add all your email addresses to your LinkedIn account now. Once you verify your email, then go and select which one will be your "primary" and display it in your Contacts section.

Tip #57

Security

Unfortunately, there are cybercriminals on all platforms today. There are fake accounts, breaches, and hacked accounts. LinkedIn does a good job of fighting these off, but we also have a personal responsibility to be diligent to protect ourselves.

Stay on top of the security of your LinkedIn account. Here are a few things you can do:

- Sign up for two-step verification for a more secure log-in
- Verify your profile with your government-issued ID ("About this profile")
- Be selective when it comes to your connections
- Change your password every 90 days
- Download your profile and account data periodically
- Save a PDF version of your profile periodically
- Don't click on links in messaging unless you know they are safe
- Sign up for an "Open Profile" if you have a premium account. Let people know you wish to be contacted only via LinkedIn and that you have this feature selected (and now, with this, you can decide to hide your email address on the platform).

Sandra's Sidebar: Take digital security seriously. Every month, I get a panic note from a client whose account was hacked or compromised.

Action Steps: Add two-step verification and profile verification right now!

Mark your calendar to check all security settings every quarter. New security features and settings are routinely being rolled out.

Tip #58

Expand with Character

Expand your descriptions and use more words and characters. LinkedIn will occasionally change character counts, so you may have a shorter entry because of an old character count. Here are some of the most relevant counts for your profile as of this writing.

- **Headline**: 220 characters
- **About**: 2,600 characters
- **Experience Description**: 2,000 characters
- **Experience Title**: 100 characters
- **Publication Title**; **Publication Publisher**; **Course Name**; **Project Name**; **Honor and Award Title**; **Organization Name**: 255 characters
- **Honor and Award Description**: 2,000 characters
- **Language**: 80 characters
- **Organization Position Held**: 1,000 characters
- **Organization Description**: 2,000 characters
- **Services Page About Description**: 500 characters

> **Sandra's Sidebar:** I have noticed that many people are short-changing themselves by not providing full descriptions or stories in the various profile sections. Fewer people may find and learn about your capabilities when not optimized.

Action Step. Look over your profile to see if you wish to expand any of your titles or descriptions.

Tip #59

Quality Check

The final quality check is up to you. Take a fresh look after taking a break away from your profile and make sure:

- Spelling and grammar are correct
- Personal and company content is always truthful and accurate
- The descriptions are clear–they are not confusing or overloaded with acronyms
- You write in a first-person friendly and positive tone
- You are using past tense for prior positions and present tense for current roles
- Consistently use punctuation and tenses
- Remove any duplicate profiles
- White space is apparent–no over-packed paragraphs
- Your resume (or bio) and profile are consistent with dates and content

Sandra's Sidebar: Make sure that the mobile app version of your profile looks good too. Check it after every profile update.

Action Step: Send your new profile content to a knowledgeable friend or a professional for honest feedback. Nothing beats getting the perspective from actual viewers.

Closing Tips

Tip #60

Be the Friend First

Heads up! This is the most important tip in this book. I also consider it my mantra, so it is front and center on my profile.

Your mindset matters on LinkedIn. Use the platform to build relationships. Focus on being the friend first.

Make other people feel special, appreciated, and noticed. Be the friend that you always wish you had. How do you do that on LinkedIn?

- Like and comment
- Invite people to connect with a friendly note
- Post a gratitude post
- Recommend and endorse
- Introduce people you know who should know each other
- Boast about others and not yourself
- Send a friendly message (not a sales pitch)
- Join Groups and then invite your friend into the Group
- Congratulate your contact by message or a post
- Recognize your friend or colleague's great job or new article with an @Mention on comment or post

- Write an article and share
- Celebrate a colleague
- Invite someone to an event
- Share and post about your friend's accomplishment

Action Step: Be the Friend First. All day and every day.

Be the Friend First™

Tip #61

Stay Professional

While LinkedIn is increasingly personal, I recommend you always stay professional. Yes, you can be both personal and professional at the same time. Be smart about where you draw the line. The impressions you create will affect your career, partnerships, selling, hiring, and overall business.

Being professional doesn't mean being boring. Weave your personality into your professional ideas. Be You. Anyone who wants to hire you or do business with you will be interested in you as a person, but they don't want to learn too much about you that is overly personal.

Second, think twice before sharing political or religious opinions that might be controversial or outside of your professional journey. Those opinions are more suited to X (Twitter).

It's a balancing act for everyone. Staying professional and friendly always seems to work well.

> **Sandra's Sidebar**: I recommend avoiding swearing and foul language. Too many people are turned off by that, including myself. Of course, you will decide for yourself, but I wanted to share my opinion with you. Am I old fashioned? Yup. Do I have friends and clients who do it? Yup again.

Action Step: Commit to being professional on LinkedIn. Decide what this means for you.

Tip #62

Evolving You

Your brand is ever-evolving. Your life, business, approach, vision, opportunities, and focus areas are all changing regularly.

Keep your profile updated regularly. You certainly want your profile to be updated to reflect any changes in your work experience, education, skills, or accomplishments. But what about changes in direction or focus? Yes, update your profile to describe your newest initiatives and focus areas.

> **Sandra's Sidebar**: Plan to review your profile every quarter, or even more, if you are going through a lot of changes in your career or business.

Action Step: Mark a date every three months on your calendar to do a strategic read-through of your profile and make updates. Yes, schedule it right now!

Tip #63

Slimming Down Your Profile

People can only absorb so much information. Don't make the mistake of overwhelming them with unnecessary detail. Focus your profile strategically and keep it current. Don't be afraid to delete or streamline information.

This is especially true for people who have been working for some time. You may have worked for 30 years and had 19 individual jobs at five companies. Look to merge some of those positions if it makes sense, but keep the dates and descriptions accurate. You can also reduce the descriptions in older positions within your Experience section, especially if they are no longer relevant.

Regardless of how long you have been working, delete those organizations, publications, volunteering, or certifications that no longer apply.

> **Sandra's Sidebar**: Too much information is a thing. Sometimes you just need to make cuts. Have you heard the phrase "less is more"? Before you cut out old content be sure to save a PDF copy of your profile in case you wish to use it in the future.

Action Step: Give your profile a "spring cleaning" at least once a year to align with your brand. Clear out the unnecessary content.

Tip #64

Brand Ambassador Opportunity

Has your company or manager asked you to become a brand ambassador for your employer on LinkedIn? Have they asked you to display a company banner or insert some company language into your profile?

I generally think this is a great idea. Look at this as a new visibility opportunity. Your brand and the company brand are both relevant and intertwined. Profile viewers who are interested in you may also be interested in your company. And vice versa.

Today's marketing teams are thinking about the buyer's increasingly digital journey. Today's HR departments are wise to consider the candidate's journey, which is also online. Therefore, the company employees are vital links to these strategic networks.

Problems only arise when the company wants to go overboard, and I have seen this happen. There is a balance to strike. Be yourself, but be open-minded to this opportunity.

Ultimately, you decide what goes on with your personal profile. Make sure it reflects the real you and consider adding in relevant company-branded profile elements as well.

> **Sandra's Sidebar**: I would consider it a compliment that your manager considers you and your profile an important part of the company brand. Everyone wins with a company like this. I love working with organizations that realize their team is the best part of their brand. Just make sure not to let your viewers lose sight of your personal brand.

Action Step: Consider supporting your company's efforts with LinkedIn because you can make this a positive thing for your own brand too!

Tip #65

Add a Company Page and Logo

There are over 63 million company pages on LinkedIn, according to Sprout Social. Your company or organization can increase visibility and be found from their own LinkedIn presence.

Consider creating a LinkedIn Company Page if you own your own company. This will give your company more visibility via search on both Google and LinkedIn. Also, the logo and link will appear on your profile (and on your employees' or team's profiles).

Fill in all the information, including tagline, industry, employee count, type, location, year founded, and description.

Upload the company logo and a background banner. The company logo should appear on your profile next to your title in the experience section. This is nice because the appearance is better, and the logo provides a direct link to the page.

> **Sandra's Sidebar**: LinkedIn Company Pages are critical digital real estate, and we work with our client's pages all the time. However, be aware that personal profiles are even more valuable for search, branding, visibility, networking, and building relationships in the majority of instances. Ideally, a Company Page and employee profiles are connected and work together.

Action Step: Create your company page today; or have a professional help you do it. Ask your friend or partner to view all aspects of the page as a quality check.

Tip #66

Compliance

Check your employer's social media policy to make sure you comply with their policies.

If you are working in a regulated industry, be aware of all requirements and act accordingly. In particular, the finance and legal industries typically have set regulations for social media profiles.

> **Sandra's Sidebar**: When we do our LinkedIn profile workshops with employee teams we always refer to their policies to make sure we are in alignment.

Action Step: Double-check your company's policies and follow suit.

Tip #67

Be Consistent

Make sure your professional online and offline presence is in alignment. No confusion!

Use the same headshot across the web and with your social channels for quicker brand recognition. Use similar language and images as well.

Do this so people will immediately recognize you. There will be clarity instead of confusion.

Stay consistent with your messaging and tone. Your brand voice should be the same across platforms.

Action Step: Check for brand consistency on all your channels and platforms.

BONUS TIPS

Tip #68

Display and Share Your Profile

Update your profile and then display or share it as a link, QR code, or banner.

Consider these locations to share or display your profile:

- Website (Consider adding a "follow me" or "public profile" badge)
- Bio pages
- Business card
- Presentations
- Articles or blogs
- Podcast pages
- Videos
- Twitter profile
- Google
- Facebook Page or profile
- Instagram
- Linktree
- YouTube
- Threads
- Resume
- Directory listings for your industry or city
- Online portals
- Digital profiles
- College alumni site

- Association or organization websites

Action Step: Display your profile wherever possible using your updated custom URL, a QR code, or a "follow me" banner.

Tip #69

Increase Profile Views

Are you looking for more profile views?

It's rather simple. The more active you are, the more profile views you will generate. When I say active, I mean online *and* in person.

You can expect more profile views if you are networking, calling, Zooming, emailing, speaking, meeting, or generally doing any professional activity. If you take part in an event or write an article, expect more views.

Your online LinkedIn activity will certainly pump up your views. Commenting is my number one suggestion for generating LinkedIn profile attention. Comment with meaningful insights on posts and articles. Add your opinions and viewpoint so people will want to learn more about you.

After mastering commenting, consider becoming a content creator by writing posts or articles; uploading videos and documents; or participating in lives or events.

Other actions on LinkedIn to drive views include endorsing, inviting, joining groups or events, posting, recommending, sending friendly messages, and profile viewing.

Action Step: Increase your online and offline activity. Most importantly, consider adding your insightful comments on the LinkedIn posts created by your network and industry.

Tip #70

It's Not a Tattoo!

I witness the fear. People tell me they need to wait all the time.

Some people are afraid to update their profiles because it is not yet *perfect*. They put LinkedIn on that professional pedestal.

I am urging you to forge ahead. Whatever profile updates you are making now are going to be far better than what you had on there before.

Everything can be changed again. And again.

It's not a tattoo! You can very easily make updates!

Instead, make your updates knowing you can modify them later today, tomorrow, or any day.

Action Step: Make the changes right away. Just do it.

Tip #71

Last Word for Job Seekers

Be sure to check the Jobs tab and navigate around the Preferences and Application settings.

Look for options around communicating with recruiters. You can save a resume and specific demographic data. Check these options out and decide if it will be beneficial for you to do so.

Example: If you are a veteran, let recruiters know in the demographic settings.

Action Step: Take a comprehensive look at the Jobs tab Preferences and Application settings and adjust them accordingly. LinkedIn makes regular updates, so put this in your calendar to do regularly.

MORE HELP IS HERE

How to Do Everything Recommended in this Book

It's not practical to show all the exact "how-to's" in this book because LinkedIn changes frequently. You will learn more about the "what to do" and "why to do it" here.

So, there are two ways that I have developed to share the how-to aspect.

First, I made a video on how to do the profile edits.

Second, I listed all the how-to links for you. These are straight from LinkedIn.

Finally, you will receive examples for About essays, headlines, and banners along with About essay prompts.

All this information is available to you via the *Jumpstart Your LinkedIn Profile* **Companion Guide**, which I will update periodically.

Here is the link to access.

https://bit.ly/profilejump

Table of Contents for Companion Guide

A. Profile Editing Video–How to Make Profile Edits

B. Headline Examples

C. Two About Section Examples–Using 5H and 2H Formats

D. About Essay Prompts if You Feel Stuck

E. Special Resource Links for You

F. LinkedIn Help Links

G. Example Banners

Thank you.

https://bit.ly/profilejump

ABOUT THE AUTHOR

Sandra Long is a leading global independent LinkedIn consultant, instructor, and speaker. She is the author of two bestselling books, **LinkedIn for Personal Branding**, and with co-author Bill Soroka, **Supercharge Your Notary Business with LinkedIn**.

Sandra was the first speaker to share her ideas about LinkedIn on the TEDx stage in 2019. Her talk was called LinkedIn Community: A Superpower Hiding in Plain Sight.

She is also the President of Post Road Consulting LLC. The company's clients include sales teams, companies, executives, event organizers, HR teams, associations, universities, and ERGs (employee resource groups) and BRGs (business resource groups).

Sandra is a graduate of the University of Rochester. She is a professional member of the *National Speakers Association* and a board member of the New England chapter.

For fun, she enjoys snow and water sports, long walks, cooking, family, and friends.

Based near Boston, Sandra flies out of Logan Airport. Contact Sandra at Sandra@PostRoadConsulting.com or on LinkedIn for speaking, consulting, training, or large quantity book orders.

BEFORE WE PART WAYS

Your LinkedIn profile is not just a digital resume; it's a canvas where your professional story and portfolio unfold for your connections. It's where opportunities find their way to your inbox, where collaborations begin, and where your brand shines.

Remember, you're not just another profile in the sea of digital faces; you're a beacon for your unique blend of skills, experiences, values, and aspirations. Be the profile that stands out in this vast sea, the one they remember, and the person they can't wait to connect with.

Here's how we can keep the conversation going:

Connect on LinkedIn: I would be delighted to welcome you to my professional network on LinkedIn. Send an invitation to connect with a personal note so I know you've journeyed through this book with me. Connect with me here: https://www.linkedin.com/in/longsandra/.

Share Your Insights: If this book has offered you valuable insights, kindly consider sharing your experience with a review on Amazon or your other bookseller platform. Your feedback not only supports my work and helps my business, but also guides others to make informed decisions about their LinkedIn presence.

Let's Collaborate: For speaking engagements, training sessions, or bulk book purchases, reach out to me directly at Sandra@PostRoadConsulting.com. Together, we can create waves of new opportunities.

Thank you for choosing this book, for your trust, and for your time. I am honored to be a part of your LinkedIn journey and professional network.

Wishing you success with every profile edit and new connection.

Printed in Great Britain
by Amazon

47866846R00056